Impact of COVID–19 on the Hospitality Industry: Climbing Towards Recovery

Impact of COVID–19 on the Hospitality Industry: Climbing Towards Recovery

Kahkasha Wahab

ELIVA PRESS

Published by Eliva Press
Email: info@elivapress.com
Website: www.elivapress.com

ISBN: 978-1-63648-281-1

Contents

Abstract:

This comprehensive research has been undertaken to evaluate the impact of COVID-19 in the hotel and restaurant industry. Amid temporary closures, introducing drive-thru, pick-up, third party deliveries, implementation of new technologies, and finally reopening, the restaurant industry and gone through ups and downs. Many restaurants could not afford to return to business and many lost track and employees. To evaluate the impact of COVID-19, this paper has discussed the three vital stages of the recent life of the restaurant - "Pre COVID-19", "During COVID-19" and "After COVID-19". The descriptive research has been conducted on independent restaurants to shed light on how COVID-19 has impacted them and also suggested the possible effects of survival. A variety of key themes have arisen from the findings. Firstly, the reopened hotels and restaurants workers have laid off or furloughed more than 50% of workers in Bangladesh. According to a National Restaurant Association study of the economic impact of the coronavirus crisis, the entire restaurant industry is forecast to sustain $240 billion in losses by the end of 2020. Secondly, contrary to previous research, we find that many small companies are financially weaker than before. Therefore, the purpose of this analysis is also to explore the potential effect of the COVID-19 in the hospitality sector due to the restricted movement, summarize the lessons that were learned from other similar epidemics and global crises, and exploring the potential steps towards recovery.

Introduction:

The unprecedented pandemic, caused by Novel Coronavirus, SARS-CoV-2 (COVID -19) is causing a devastating effect on the hospitality industry from the very beginning of 2020 and placed tremendous strain on the healthcare system. The entire hospitality industry felt this previously unknown disease had an immediate impact and the restaurant industry has faced a tremendous shift. In addition to its impact on public health, COVID-19 has had a considerable economic impact on the restaurants and hotels throughout the world. While the restaurant industry has proven agile in coming up with new ways to continue operating

3

with dining rooms closed to customers, the announcement of allowing reopening sent a light of hope through those dark times. Now as the world is reopening there is a growing debate over procedures to keep people safe and secure.

The recent outbreak of Coronavirus has led to a global panic owing to its fatality. On 31 December 2019, pneumonia of an uncertain origin found in Wuhan, China, was first confirmed to China's WHO country office. 41 patients with identified infections from a novel coronavirus (COVID-19) were hospitalized in China in early January 2020 (Huang et al., 2020). From that now, the incidence of infection increased by community spread, and reported cases reached 60 million (with more than 1.41 million deaths) in over 200 countries by November 25, 2020 (ECDC 2020). The exact overall number of cases in most countries remains uncertain, as research and testing are minimal. With no vaccination to avoid the disease and minimal medical services accessible to cure it, many countries reacted with various types of non-pharmaceutical interventions (NPI), including lockdown (home confinement, voluntary/necessary quarantine), social distancing (vulnerable or whole populations), closing of schools/universities and non-essential enterprises/workplaces, termination or postponing of international sports events, such as Olympics, restricting the gathering of people in the public places over a certain number, etc. as a measure to control the spread of the virus over the time. The epidemic has infected nearly every aspect of the supply chain of hospitality within countries. Many sections of the supply chain, such as catering and laundry systems, quickly felt the effects of canceled activities, closed hotels and shut down attractions. Restaurants have had to close, though a move to take-away / delivery sales in some countries enabled some to continue operations.

This paper has two overlapping goals against such a background of a fast-changing global pandemic. First, to objectively study the past literature on the effect on the global hospitality and restaurant industry of recent epidemics/pandemics and equate such incidents to certain forms of global crises. This section also looks at whether the COVID-19 pandemic was an unknown or unaccountable risk. Recognizing that the impact on global hospitality has only just begun, the second objective is to summarize early estimates of the economic damage over 2020 and beyond, classifying the impact into Pre-COVID, During-COVID, and After-COVID stages. Owing to the enormous complexity, these early projections are objectively tested against appropriate epidemiological modeling and public safety scenarios for transportation and public meeting constraints. Finally, the paper looks at how the COVID-19 pandemic will affect the hospitality culture, the environment, and restaurants, and some of the main work needed to recognize those improvements and lead to a more viable post-pandemic guest market. As soon as the epidemic will be under control, there would be an impulse for everyone to return to business as normal, even to overcompensate with making more rapid development for losses.

To date, different research works on the impact of COVID-1 on the hospitality industry have been undertaken, the findings of which are:

- Impact to the travel industry 9 times worse than 9/11. (Tourism Economics)
- 50 percent revenue decline (projected) for the entirety of 2020 (Oxford Economics)
- Eight in 10 hotel rooms are empty. (STR)
- 2020 is projected to be the worst year on record for hotel occupancy. (CBRE)
- The forecasted occupancy rate for 2020 is worse than 1933 during the Great Depression. (CBRE)
- 70 percent of hotel employees laid off or furloughed. (Oxford Economics and Hotel Effectiveness)
- $2.4 billion in weekly lost wages due to the crisis (Oxford Economics and Hotel Effectiveness)
- Nearly 3.9 million total hotel-supported jobs lost since the crisis began (Oxford Economics)

Past pandemics, epidemics, global crisis, etc. and its effect on the hospitality industry:

It is necessary to remember that in the past, the global hospitality industry was subject to a large variety of crises. Around 2000 and 2015, significant disrupting incidents include the terrorist attacks of September 11 (2001), the epidemic of Severe Acute Respiratory Syndrome (SARS), the global economic crisis that occurred in 2008/2009, and the epidemic of 2015 Middle East Respiratory Syndrome (MERS) are just to name a few remarkable ones. All of these also contributed to a longer-term downturn in global tourism and hospitality growth and some of them are not even noticeable, with just SARS (-0.4%) and the global economic recession (-4.0%) contributing to decreases in foreign arrivals (World Bank 2020a, 2020b). The restaurant industry, in particular, had very little impact on these global crises and the amount of loss was easy to recover. This may imply that as a method, the restaurant industry in Bangladesh was immune to external shocks. There is, moreover, ample proof that the COVID-19 pandemic's effects and regeneration on tourism, hospitality, events, and restaurants would be unprecedented. However, several warnings have been issued that pandemics posed a major threat to tourism, hospitality, and society (Gössling, 2002; Hall, 2006, 2020; Page & Yeoman, 2007; Scott & Gössling, 2015) and to health researchers (Bloom & Cadarette, 2019; Fauci & Morens, 2012), as well as to government agencies (National Academies of Science , Engineering and Medicine, 2017, 2018) and institutions (Jonas, 2014; World Bank).

What are the hotels doing to overcome the loss incurred by COVID-19?

The restaurant industry has been struck hard by the COVID-19 pandemics, with the government of different countries, including Bangladesh, imposing that restaurants should function only by take-out or delivery. Restaurants and some of the iconic fine dine restaurants that have never adopted delivering service before, quickly embraced home delivery and taking away models to satisfy consumers and maintain market stability through this tough period. Several restaurants have started turning parking spaces into a temporary drive-thru and have updated their menu based on their current inventory, including products that are convenient to delivery. That has reduced running expenses. Apart from this, many people have utilized this time to refurbish the restaurant and tried to bring in new business ideas and models. Such as:

- **Adopting technology:** The emergence of coronavirus has expedited the development and application of technologies in the restaurant industry like never before. Robots are introduced to reduce human to human interaction, kiosks are also widely established in the major points where previously kiosks were not found. Remote employment is now today's standard. And such a people-centered sector as hospitality faces a spike in telecommuting, due to advancements and technologies. In reality, without even being there, hoteliers will control any of the hotel processes. Cloud-based Property Management Systems allow them to manage all activities from anywhere at any time. Drone technology in delivery foods in creating potentiality. Moreover, technology is now widely used to ensure hygiene of foods.
- **Study current health and safety standards, protocols, and procedures:** Given the infectious existence of the virus, it is important that proper health and safety measures are in effect, especially for hotels that depend on in-person experiences. Hoteliers should promote appropriate health and safety measures in these contexts, which might include:
    - Pay services self-service.
    - Orders through Smartphone Devices.
    - Non-contact support and delivery to order.
    - Additional hand sanitizer stationed in the entrances and exits.
    - Discouraging unnecessary gatherings at the workplace.
    - Readiness to meet cuts in personnel.

  Hoteliers need to track the health status of workers carefully, and take appropriate steps to ensure that the illness does not spread.
- **Making sure details on coronavirus is correct:** The available data on coronavirus is not always right, because new research is continually emerging. Hoteliers should

take special caution to exchange accurate facts and not lead to the spread of disinformation to clients and employees. Information from reliable outlets such as the Centers for Disease Control and Prevention and other reputable health care professionals should be read, exchanged, or uploaded.

- **Using this time to repair and refurbish hotels:** Coronavirus pandemic doesn't mean restaurants shut their doors and are just waiting for the end of this time. It is a great chance to catch up and get stronger. If it's a casual redesign or finishing a restaurant development program, no better time to do so. To start with, one should make a list of products, anything and anything that needs to be fixed, do a maintenance inventory, and check pantry systems, railings and balcony tests, elevators, life protection checks, pool systems, make sure all lights are off, and so on. Many hotels and restaurants have been found cleaning the restaurant premises, A/C scrubbing, fabric cleaning, sheets, reaching behind bed frames, sweeping behind walls/mirrors, and vacuuming.

Comparison between Pre-COVID and after COVID-19

- Many hotels and restaurants have replaced their items, for example, many restaurants are not selling groceries instead of casual dining to sustain in the market.
- Many are not paying their employees and many employees are losing their job.
- Introduced delivery services.

Tech threatens restaurants and hospitality sectors — pressing these businesses to embrace technologies or to face falling behind. The fear of losing human contact was one of the main challenges for the hospitality industry regarding technology adoption. With the emergence of the novel Coronavirus, caused by COVID - 19, people have started to fear human interactions and human touch. The wide use of technology has already made a tremendous impact on the foodservice industry. That might mean reassessing the entire experience of the restaurant. And also to potentially redefine hospitality, a daunting thing designed on the idea throughout an industry. Whereas the Americans take steps such as sniffing, eliminating phone calls on-site sessions, and pushing doors with shoulders rather than hands, fast-food places follow businesses such as cruise ships, airlines, and car hire firms to see their activities disrupted by the exponential development of the epidemic. It's particularly difficult for the foodservice industry. Before the advent of this Coronavirus, people thought that Facetime and Zoom things were okay but the human touch was their all-time preferred to get the feeling of warmth. The virus has now started to shift these feelings into fear where people are now more comfortable in Facetimes, ordering foods through online sites, home delivery, and pick-up. With the growing fear of human beings for this virus and increased consciousness of hygiene, it is estimated that it would take a long time to come back to the previous life, leaving many restaurants to shut down.

Post COVID-19 will discuss how the restaurants will come up with the losses and in what can be the possible ways that they can adapt to come back.

Following COVID-19 lockdowns, customer behavior in an environment parallels pre- and post-crisis patterns that focus on the restaurant industry. An online research conducted by Simon-Kucher & Partners (2020) addresses subjects such as distribution expectations (including 3rd party platforms) focused on customer segments, deep insights into market segments valuing various order and pick-up networks, and ability to pay. The study was developed on the basis of a survey conducted by 647 restaurant consumers representing US demographics. Main Research results showed that:

Home cooked meals are the greatest challenge from COVID-19 lockdowns in restaurants – customers are expecting to eat 37% of meals at home relative to 33% before COVID-19

Willingness to compensate and switch to equivalent or higher channel rates – If customers eat out, they plan to visit healthy restaurants (e.g. salad/sandwich) or high-quality restaurants (e.g. fast casual burger)

Customers expect to buy more regularly from post-lockdown apps/websites – Consumers aim to buy 25% of their meals from apps and websites after restrictions have been removed, compared with 21% before COVID-19.

Delivery and curbside pick-up consumption channels most likely to grow after lock-downs are lifted – Consumers intend to receive 14% of meals through delivery and 8% of meals through post-COVID-19 curbside pick-up, compared to 12% and 5%, respectively, pre-COVID-19. Increasingly, just 45% of customers have purchased food by distribution whereas 70% of delivery orders go to a third party portal.

To see the changes from the Pre-COVID, During COVID and Post-COVID changes in the hotels and restaurants, a closer look at the changes are seen from 6 viewpoints. They are shortly described below:

1. **Operations:**

   As the COVID-19 is making the population collectively suffer from its contagion, restaurants and hotels can bring in new changes in their operations to come back to business and climb towards recovery. Previously, the basic COVID-19 hygiene principles were not regularly seen in the restaurants. But the emergence of coronavirus has already brought and still bringing substantial changes in the operations. Such as, wearing gloves and masks, maintaining a 6 feet gap between the customers, hand sanitizing, etc. Such steps that the restaurants are now taking to reopen their business are:

   - Mandating use of gloves and masks into the restaurant premises
   - Support consumers to retain strong protection and social distance from infections by:
     Discontinuation of facilities, such as salad bars, buffets and beverage service stations that involve the usage of specific utensils or dispensers for consumers.
   - Finding incentives to stimulate customer spacing while in line for service or check-out according to applicable State or local requirements.
   - Discouraging consumers from taking dogs into shops or waiting rooms – except for service animals.

Having already reported, the effect of COVID-19 would have a longer lasting influence nowhere but in the industry's table service market. While some will return as loyal customers and pour support and loyalty, it is expected, at least initially, that a larger number will not. Table service restaurants ought to think about how to handle the issues that clients are expected to pose and try their utmost to resolve them right away.

According to Toby Malbec (2020) such ideas and methods for resolving obstacles may include:

- Increased distance between tables and/or decomposition of larger rooms in smaller parts
- Greater exposure (and visibility) to hygienic goods on tables and in public spaces, such as wipes and sanitizers
- Cutlery, glassware and plates for customer healthcare cleaned at the table side (or brought to the table packed).
- Removal of salt and chili shakers and supply either in packages or on request
- Table coverings removed over meal plates
- Pay-at-table features to prevent credit card transactions to a cloud
- Offer e-receipts instead of print
- Digital menu platforms or anti-microbial screen tablets, instead of paper menus

Although the end date for such emergency initiatives remains uncertain, restaurants will start taking action through the closure to adapt to the "new normal" and plan to remain ready when the US recovers from this crisis.

2. Technology

It has been a while since the restaurants are trying to adapt technology in every facet of their services. We have already seen the use of robots, kiosks, drones, etc in the food industry. However, the device more useful than ever before in the restaurant industry during COVID-19 is - thermal health checks at the entrance of the guests and staff. Hotels and restaurants do their employees a quick health check as they return to work. Just as the airports and hospitals are performing, we might expect employers to provide nervous employee masks as well as checking temperatures as employee's clock in. Time Clocks would be able to take a temperature and by any biometric means as part of the clocking phase, including the potential to warn the manager not to clock in with a high temperature.

The COVID-19 outcome would result in technical changes, mainly based on 'contactless' or 'less-contact' technologies, having an integral role in reshaping market and consumer behavior.

Some of the more progressive restaurant brands have been preaching for many years the importance of visibility of the supply chain and the ability to track products literally from farm to back door to plate. The infrastructure to do so exists, but it has frightened away all but the most cautious of deployment and start-up times and costs to do so. The goal and the promise of the GS1 initiative is to provide a common "language" and method for tracking and reporting on all products from their point of creation (or growth) to the production facility, to the warehouse, to the broad liner, and finally to the restaurant. Through labeling each container with a special code (GTIN), in case a foodborne disease is detected in a drug, we will practically be able to trace down to the farmer or even the field. Today, the technology exists; it actually takes tremendous cooperation from food service operators and distributors to decide to comply with requirements, customize their devices to accommodate GTIN quantities, and launch them.

These are some of the restaurant technologies that could intensify in a post-COVID-19 environment.

- **Online food ordering is a necessity and will be stable for an indefinite period**

Since online ordering services have been influential in stopping many restaurants from shutting down, beginning here makes sense. Regardless of the design of the venue, establishments that did not have this product until had to change their market models immediately to sell delivery facilities, whether a fast-casual or fine dining. Several QSRs have had to go on a recruiting binge after the shutdown to meet a huge amount of customers' online requests. This pattern would just go steady, if not see an upsurge, because after the COVID-19 epidemic consumers would already be more careful about dining out in crowded areas.

- **Tech-based Supply Systems**

With the fast-growing online restaurant delivery segment, developments in modern distribution technologies should also be made targeted at cheaper, more efficient and better hygienic activities. During the current outbreak, we have seen how drones and robots are being used to deliver medical supplies in healthcare environments, since the sudden pandemic has led to companies working on these technologies speeding up their tests. Chinese startup Pony.ai has recently unveiled a logistics program using automated cars in California. Sooner or expected, restaurants too will catch up on these distribution innovations.

- **Contactless and Cashless drive-thru**

The goal of most restaurant businesses in the future would be to eliminate human activity as far as possible. This suggests the cashier-less drive-thrus might be a real alternative. This hybrid system would involve several innovations, including profound research, perception strategies, cameras and sensors that will operate in unison to accept requests, collect purchases, and deliveries. In March 2020, Amazon has already confirmed it would carry out its 'Only Step Out' cashier-less mobile checkout systems to other stores. Similar technology could be developed for drive-thrus restaurants as well.

- **Touchless Food**

Public distancing would be brought to a whole new stage when restaurants are expected to implement contactless dining services intended to eliminate touch with employees and customers. These technologies might mean the end of physical menus, one of a restaurant's germiest surfaces, especially plastic menus. Proof exists the traces of E. Coli, S. One can find aureus (staph) on the menus, as these germs are passed from hand to hand. Instead, emerging technology might enable clients to access their own phones or tablets via menus, position an order directly from those apps, and even make payments.

- **More technology-based ways to pay online**

This takes us to the growing proliferation of modern payment systems that remove all cash and card purchases in order to restrict surface interaction. A report in the Time magazine brought out the dirty side of the currency, very simply, showing that banknotes can hold everything from marijuana to fecal matter and that a live flu virus would survive up to 17 days on its surface. Although electronic payments such as Apple Pay, Google Pay, etc., and even cryptocurrencies, have already gained ground, particularly among the younger generation, further developments are highly probable in this field.

- **Use of anti-microbial screens and instruments**

Studies have shown that only touch screen menus bear contagious germs, in comparison to traditional menus. Restaurants around there are many other apps that include touch-solutions and POS equipment. Yet as we step towards an environment where the rule is minimal touch, restaurants would be required to adopt anti-microbial screens and apps. There are organizations who have already developed these pathogen resistance techniques and in the coming days, this will rapidly gain momentum.

- **Rise of companies with clean technology**

COVID-19 is a zoonotic disease and is reported to have spread from animal to human consumption via feed. In the aftermath of this pandemic, as a safer alternative, consumers would increasingly turn towards plant-based foods, propelling sustainable technology firms. Plant-based protein to clean meat was still being celebrated as the 2020 theme, but work on these meat substitutes is expected to expedite after the coronavirus outbreak. Restaurants, on the other side, are now eager to introduce more healthy meat to their selection.

- **Mobile applications for hygiene and sterilization**

This outbreak has made restaurant operators top priority in terms of hygiene and sanitation. New technology for introducing and monitoring robust sanitization procedures, whether in front of the building, back of the building or through distribution phases, will soon be making a grand entry into the restaurant industry. Top universities and tech firms are also working to develop applications to help monitor the transmission of contagious diseases, which can also be beneficial for companies.

It can be tricky for all companies to move forward during the COVID-19 pandemic. The restaurants must be highly receptive to their customers' preferences and concerns. Adopting strict hygiene practices and investing in the right equipment will help the restaurant keep ahead of the curve and get back their beloved clients to the table

3. Human resources:

For more than five decades, the effect COVID-19 has made on small and large companies is something that has rarely been experienced before. America's closing has effectively set a stop on activity in the hospitality sector. It has pushed other organizations to adopt plans for the work from home (WFH). Historical histories of jobless claims have rendered it a daunting task to manage human resources. The Trump Administration lifted the travel alert to "level 4" on January 30, and the travel ban came into force on February 2nd in the US with inbound travelers from China flying within 14 days (Corkery & Karni, 2020). Instead came new transportation controls, representing a significant change in the global economy. On March 18, Marriott announced it had begun the process of furloughing tens of thousands of associates (Karmin, 2020). On March 17th Hilton announced it would close most of their hotels (Ollila, 2020; Reigler, 2020). This prompted the eventual

15

closing of several of the hotels when governments, states and municipal authorities imposed new public safety advisories.

The unemployment reports have soared with the major closings in the service sector. On 9 April, the week-end survey ending 4 April 2020 had 6.6 million initial claims (adjusted for seasonality) (Labor Agency, 2020). This was a decline of 261,000 claims, with 6.8 million adjusted claims compared to the week before (Labor Department, 2020).

The total claims over the last three weeks are over 16 million. Comparing such figures to the 151 million workers actually reported in the last monthly jobs survey, this implies that in three weeks the U.S. lost 10 percent of the population (Franck & Schoen, 2020).

The biggest segment of the economy that has experienced work cuts, diving deep into the unemployment statistics, falls from recreation and hospitality.

An analysis undertaken by Oxford Economics breaks down the state-by - state employment loss in the lodging sector, predicting an estimated 44 per cent work loss (American Hotel & Lodging Group, 2020; Asmelash & Cooper, 2020).

This is the time when training the employees come into play. When this situation comes to an end, we will need to get back soon. So, this time is to train and educate the team on the skills it will need. Of starters, sales management may continue to develop partnerships with companies and not 'offer' – often new sales management will be more of an order-taker, not having served through the 2008-2009 financial crisis or the 9/11 terror attacks. The HR can also offer educational courses online as a tool to hold staff involved.

Here are a few ways to maintain social distancing in the workplace:

- Staggered work shift
- Limit number of employees in break rooms, restrooms, meeting rooms, etc.
- Increase physical space between employees at the worksite

- Implementation of flexible meeting and travel options (e.g., postpone non-essential meetings or events)
- Deliver services remotely (e.g., phone, video, or web)
- Deliver products through curbside pick-up or delivery

So, HR and learning leaders can utilize this time to formulate a complete inventory of their learning offerings by type of delivery and to focus on how virtual learning is optimized. The first move in many situations is to initiate some form of governance feature, mostly a cross-functional team made up of members from HR business associates, organizational development representatives, IT and development implementation associates. When part of a wider post-COVID-19 initiative, this unit will also collaborate alongside the larger Business Continuity unit at the organization to develop preparation and HR strategies based on maintaining a healthy workforce.

4. **Financial Performance**:

U.S. restaurants are spinning from COVID-19 impact. A day, in reaction to the outbreak, many local and state officials shutter bars and restaurants to dine-in customers. At least 25 states have ordered closures as of this writing (March 25). However, most restaurants will still serve food through take-out, delivery, or drive-through. This helps eateries to retain certain sales thus helping to curb COVID-19 distribution.

A new survey of the Virginia Restaurant, Lodging & Travel Association conducted by Lindsey Kennett (2020) shows widespread and immense financial damage due to COVID-19. The study reports that the restaurant and food service companies in Virginia have suffered $1.3 billion in revenue in April alone. Eric Terry, President of the Virginia Restaurant, Lodging & Travel Association, said it's an unprecedented downward trend across the Commonwealth. He added that "We've never seen this kind of impact on the restaurant industry, even in 9/11 and all the

17

other things, and you know, probably never see it again," The association also released a nationwide effects study of the restaurant sector and discovered that 237,000 workers have either been laid off or furloughed, suggesting three out of four jobs are gone.

The following charts will illustrate the comparison of Pre-COVID, During COVID and recovery stage of the restaurants from the damage caused by COVID-19:

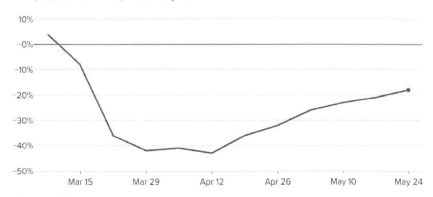

Overall restaurant transactions
Compared to the same period last year

SOURCE: NPD Group's Crest Performance Alerts, which use geo-tracking data for 70 quick service, fast casual, midscale and casual dining chains.

Figure 1: Overall Restaurant transactions

As states around the world revive their markets, following stay-at - home mandates, the restaurant sector is displaying signs of growth, and social distancing initiatives led profits to plunge. The NPD Company, which monitors transactions for 70 fast-service, fast-casual, and full-service restaurant chains, reported that transactions declined just 18 percent over the week ended May 24.During the week ending 12 April, restaurant transactions reached their nadir. On Saturday, April 11, the IRS started to deposit the first round of stimulus checks into bank accounts for Americans. The extra cash seems to have given a boost to the restaurant industry as consumers who had grown tired of cooking were looking to spend their $1,200.

Some states, such as Georgia, began allowing dining rooms to reopen by early May, despite concerns over a second wave of Covid-19 cases. The move further elevated restaurant sales especially for higher-margin items such as alcohol.

Currently the NPD Group is reporting that about 320,000 establishments in the U.S. are permitted to provide a certain amount of on-site dining. But while many restaurants are allowed to reopen their dining rooms with limited capacity, some move more slowly, out of concern for their clients and staff. On the other hand, independent restaurants have a tougher path to recovery, with as many as 30 percent never expected to reopen their gates once more.

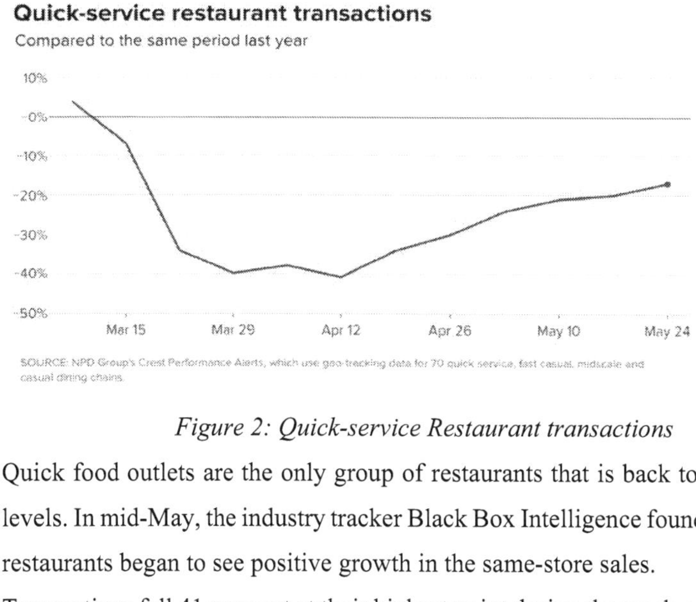
Quick-service restaurant transactions
Compared to the same period last year
10%
0%
-10%
-20%
-30%
-40%
-50%
Mar 15
Mar 29
Apr 12
Apr 26
May 10
May 24
SOURCE: NPD Group's Crest Performance Alerts, which use geo-tracking data for 70 quick service, fast casual, midscale and casual dining chains.

Figure 2: Quick-service Restaurant transactions

Quick food outlets are the only group of restaurants that is back to pre-pandemic levels. In mid-May, the industry tracker Black Box Intelligence found that fast-food restaurants began to see positive growth in the same-store sales.

Transactions fell 41 per cent at their highest point during the week of April 12. The accessibility of drive-thru lanes, which typically taken into account for about 70 per cent of pre-crisis transactions, probably helped sales of the segment during lockdowns. And fast-food restaurants are recognized for their cheap deals, which could make them more accessible to customers after the U.S. economy was upset by the pandemic. Even though revenues of the category bounce back, traffic to fast-food restaurants stays under control, suggesting shoppers spend more on restaurants like McDonald's and Yum Brands' Taco Bell during their infrequent visits. In the week ending May 24, purchases dropped by 17 percent.

Full-service restaurant transactions
Compared to the same period last year

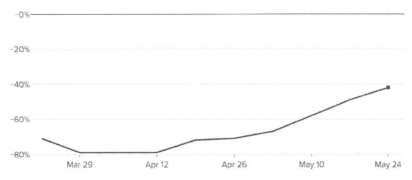

SOURCE: NPD Group's Crest Performance Alerts, which use geo-tracking data for 70 quick service, fast casual, midscale and casual dining chains. Data for weeks ending March 8 and March 15 not available for full-service restaurants.

Figure 3: Full-service Restaurant transactions

The pandemic struck restaurants full-service the worst. For the first time, closures in the dining room forced many to pivot to delivery and takeout. Others simply chose to keep their doors closed for the length of the lockdown. Transactions at full-service restaurants plummeted 79 percent for three weeks in a row between the end of March and mid-April. The transactions of the segment fell less than 70 percent during the week ended May 3, since states began rolling out stay-at - home orders. While several governors encourage consumers to return to dining rooms with reduced space, full-service restaurant purchases are still down 42 percent from the week ended May 24.

To best imagine the incredible impact of the closure, below are several of the restaurant industry shares about the:

- On March 25, Yum Brands, owning Pizza Hut, KFC, and Taco Bell, among others, announced the temporary closure of 7,000 restaurants around the globe, including 1,000 US Pizza Hut Express stores.
- Nationally the big fast food chains removed their dining rooms and switched to carryout, pickup, and drive-thru. That includes McDonald's, Wendy's, Arby's, Chick-fil-A, Chipotle, Panera Bread, Shake Shack, Subway, and Starbucks.
- D'Artagnan Foods, a premium meat manufacturer, notes that restaurants are 70 percent of its market.
- Lucas Papierniak, the supplier of seafood said, "Business has just ended" and he expects that restarting his supply chain will take three months.
- Restaurants are rated as 55 percent of their revenue by Soom Foods (tahini manufacturer and a former Forbes 30 under 30).
- As a consequence of coronavirus-related restaurant closings, farmers discarded milk and split eggs, reducing demand for their food.
- The Regional Restaurant Association reported revenue worth more than $25 billion have already been diverted to the sector.

It continues to remain unforeseen how far that will end up taking the restaurant industry from the covid-19 downturn. Or the restaurant industry should keep the battle.

5. Guest Aptitude:

It's no mystery that the food service sector – and the hospitality business as a whole – are significantly affected by government-imposed control initiatives. But several restaurateurs have been able to change their business model and provide more versatile, pandemic-friendly dining choices for their clients. This also culminated in a rise in choices for taking-away and delivery service, not only from short food or fast-casual restaurants, but also from high-end restaurants. Some restaurants have adopted comprehensive health and safety laws to safeguard both their employees and their customers – from procurement to planning and operation. In the USA, Europe and China, food service operators such as McDonald's and Starbucks came up with contactless pick-up services in which consumers did not have to make any contact with the workers. When several foreign franchises including McDonald's, Subway, KFC and Burger King have chosen to shut stores entirely, local, regional companies have an increasing chance to fill the void. These companies are more agile and flexible because they employ fewer employees (often from the same family), and can therefore react faster to serve local customers. These customers are likely to spread the message across their surrounding people, further strengthening the excellence of these companies and establishing a loyal customer base that will probably stick around well after the dust has settled.

6. **Ambiance**:

Restaurants are now developing new and exciting ways to give their customers a unique eating experience, while ensuring that all social distancing guidelines are maintained. Physical evidence is one of the major service characteristics that is necessary to build customer loyalty in terms of restaurants and hotels. The customer and guests believe what they see. So to sustain in the business during this pandemic, many restaurants are trying to reflect their effort of maintaining pandemic safety rules through physical evidence. The examples of a few unique ways that the restaurants are adapting/ can adapt to win against the battle of Coronavirus are:

- Face shield, masks and gloves are seen to be used by waiters and waitresses and chefs at the restaurant to reflect safety and precautionary measures adapted by the restaurant.
- In the age of coronavirus, a Dutch restaurant called Mediamatic ETEN has come up with an idea of how to offer classy outdoor dining: small glass cabins built for two or three people, creating intimate cocoons on a public patio.

- Spanish bars and pubs have glass partitions mounted on the table to support the guests converse whilst keeping a safe and healthy distance
- People are seen eating between the plastic partitions, set up to reduce any spread of COVID-19, in Penguin Eat Shabu in Bangkok.
- Even in the developing countries, restaurants are now mandated the use of hand sanitizers at the entrances of the restaurant and general stores. The kids are now taught to use hand sanitizers as a part of their daily food routine.

7. **Revolutions:** The USA's restaurant sector confronts the arguably toughest structural challenge. While the COVID-19 shutdown decreases transmitting risk, it has also culminated in sales falling to zero, with businesses unable to find the cash to pay their workers and make rent. Maybe the pandemic only reveals the flaws that were always there. Restaurants around the world are being forced out of business. Nonetheless, many thousands that closed "temporarily" when the first lockdown instructions were issued eventually confirmed they probably couldn't afford to reopen. For example, in New York City, local institutions like the Paris Bar in Manhattan and the Lucky Strike in Soho have closed for good. So many hotels and restaurants have planned not to come back to business again.

On the other hand, there are some hotels and restaurants that have decided to transform their services. Consumers moving to small farmers for their berries, plants, and meat and dairy goods is one of the main changes. While grocery stores suffered extreme supply shortages, farms have been able to offer a constant stream of fresh goods to local shoppers.

Many local farms now offer quick-turnaround delivery or contactless collection (with impressively short lead times), which has been a major advantage for those at risk or who are quarantined at home. On the other side, grocery stores have been unable to keep up with the competition, leaving many for weeks, if at all, without an adequate distribution alternative. Thus, many restaurants have transformed their services into local grocery stores for supplying fresh foods and vegetables that are ready to cook.

Findings & Discussions:

The findings of this paper is summarized in the following table:

Situations:	Pre- COVID -19	During– COVID - 19	After COVID-19
Operations:			
1. Increased use of Masks and Gloves:	The use of masks was not much found among the restaurant and hotel staff, however, chefs had to wear gloves for the maintenance of hygiene protocol.	The service providers are seen putting on gloves and masks throughout the food processing and delivery time. The guests and customers are also found wearing masks and gloves.	Whether the coronavirus goes completely away through a vaccine, the experts are saying that it will still take a few more years to get back to the old normal life, without masks and gloves.
2. Maintaining 6 feet gap:	6 feet gap was not prevalent before the emergence of the coronavirus. It was neither prevalent among the customers nor	6 feet gap and social distancing has been mandated through the emergence of COVID-19. As a result, the restaurants have	New innovative ideas are constantly emerging to renovate the restaurant layouts that will provide the customers and guests to enjoy the

	among the restaurant staff.	increased distance between tables and/or decomposition of larger rooms in smaller parts.	food by maintaining strict social distancing to curb the spread of Coronavirus.
3. Use of soaps and hand-sanitizers:	Use of soaps in the toilets and washroom of every restaurants have always been very common.	The coronavirus pandemic has increased the wide use of hand sanitizers, alcohol-based hand rubs and hygiene practices like washing hands using soap for at least 20 seconds. These hygiene practices were not as strictly followed as after the emergence of COVID-19.	The use of hand rubs, soaps and hand-sanitizers are expected to be continued for an unprecedented time.
Technology:			
1. Use of technologies:	The restaurants were trying to bring in new	The implementation of new technologies in the food industry	Top universities and tech firms are also working to

	technological innovations into their service to attract more tech-friendly customers. We have already seen the use of robots, kiosks, drones, etc. in the food industry but the purpose was not to become contactless or cashless.	is now mainly because of going cashless and contactless. Thermal health checks at the entrance of the guests and staff is an appeared necessity. Online food ordering applications are getting focus. Use of anti-microbial screens and instruments are used now.	develop applications to help monitor the transmission of contagious diseases and developing more contactless and cashless services.
2. Third-party technologies:	Uber Eats, Foodpanda, Doordash, etc. third party food delivery systems were more popularly used to deliver foods at the door of the customers.	As food delivery system is the only common way to consume food from outside, the restaurants are developing their own independent apps and services to deliver foods. That	The restaurants will bring new and innovative ideas to deliver food. The use of drones and robots instead of motorbike deliveries can be found in future as people will prefer

		is, they are using their own channels instead of third party channels.	to go human contactless.
Human Resources:			
1. Percentage of Employees laid off:	A study conducted by S. Lock (2020) shows the number of employees in the restaurant industry in the United States from 2010 to 2019. The number of people employed in the U.S. restaurant industry reached 13.49 million as of May 2019.	An analysis undertaken by Oxford Economics breaks down the state-by - state employment loss in the lodging sector, predicting an estimated 44 percent has lost their work and faced job loss	More than 8 million restaurant employees across the world were laid off or furloughed. According to a National Restaurant Association analysis of economic impact of the coronavirus crisis, the entire restaurant industry is projected to sustain $240 billion in losses by the end of 2020.
2. Training:	Before the COVID-19, training were given to the staff based on their job responsibilities.	To utilize the time of closures, the restaurants are training their employees to focus	Train the employees to form marketing strategies to promote the existent resources

	They were trained to perform jobs that they are specialized in. Such as the job of chef is to cook so he has been trained on cooking only. Whereas after the Coronavirus, chefs are required to learn other skills to cope up the responsibilities of a sick partner.	on to-go and delivery opportunities, Maintain open, proactive communication with managers, Cross-train employees to help cover for others who are absent, etc.	of the organization into some other ways. Ake the usage of social media to facilitate restaurant "reopening." Offer special items or discounts to win back customers who used to dine in.
Financial Performance:			
1. Financial loss:	Restaurant business was not going much financial hardship before the pandemic. According to a survey conducted by the National Restaurant Association, during the first three months (Jan, Feb,	The National Restaurant Association reported that the restaurants have lost $30 billion in March, and $50 billion in April.	According to a National Restaurant Association study of the economic impact of the coronavirus crisis, the entire restaurant industry is forecast to sustain $240 billion in losses by the end of 2020.

	Mar) of the pandemic the restaurant and food service industry probably lost nearly $120bn in sales.		
Guests Aptitude:			
1. Preferred mode of food consumption	Dine-in	Pick-up, Drive-thru and Delivery	Pick-up, Drive-thru and Delivery, Pre-booking, Occasional Dine-in
2. Percentage of the restaurant using their own delivery channel or third-party pick-up	Third-party (Uber Eats, Door dash, Grab, Seamless etc.)	Third-party and some restaurants introduced their own delivery network to cut costs.	If the preferred mode of food consumption remains limited to pick-up, drive-thru and home delivery, then the restaurants will introduce their own delivery networks, like Domino's and Pizza Hut had been doing.
Ambiance:			
1. Physical evidence:	Apart from food, interior and exterior décor, banners,	Embedded floor marks to keep a safe and healthy	The sanitizers in the tables, waiters wearing gloves and

	advertisement, music, cleanliness, etc. were the physical evidence of a good restaurant.	distance, mandating the use of hand sanitizers at the entrances, cashless and contactless services, etc. are now more preferred by health conscious people while dining.	masks, measuring body temperatures, using thermometers, maintaining social distance etc. will work as the basics of a hygiene and health conscious restaurant in the future.
2. Sitting arrangement:	Focus was more given to the comfort of the guests, furniture and outer ambiance, so that customers can sit next or close to each other, enjoy conversation while dining and have hospitable environment of warmth and care.	Substantial changes are brought in the outlays and sitting arrangements, such as small glass cabins built for two or three people, creating intimate cocoons on a public patio, eating between the plastic partitions, set up to reduce any spread of COVID-19 etc.	Re-enliven the dine-in atmosphere and search for quick and cost-effective improvements that might be made to "refresh" the dine-in experience before reopening.

3. Robots and touch-free kiosks	The use of robot, kiosk, electronic devices, etc. where limited only to perform tasks on behalf of human to reduce labor costs, save time and ensure efficiency and consistency.	The use of robots, drones, kiosks, gadgets has now a more important role to play. These are now used to go touchless and human interaction free as pandemic has taught people to fear people.	More research and studies are performed on how to develop robots and introduce these to small independent restaurants so that they can survive the battle of coronavirus.
Revolutions:			
1. Not reopening:	The restaurants used to get closed for personal crisis or inconvenience of the owners or adjacent community.	The restaurants are closed for dine-in facilities and limited only to pick-up, drive-thrus, home delivery, etc.	A study conducted by OpenTable stated that 1 in 4 restaurants won't reopen after the coronavirus pandemic. It is predicted that more than 30,000 pubs and restaurants 'may not reopen after lockdown'
2. Change in service:	Change of services was done due to the change of	Many restaurants have changes their services and moved	As a result to the irrecoverable financial damage

	preference of the customers.	from fast-food or QSR to local grocery shops, farm-based foods, etc. to sustain in the market.	caused by the COVID-19, many restaurant may not return to their old business as it will not only involve risk but also require new investment.

Conclusion:

The coronavirus pandemic, unparalleled in living history, is a worldwide epidemic. Not a single analyst or official in the government knows how long it will continue, nor what the actual economic impact would be. What we can say now is that the effects on both the economy and culture would last a really long time as people are afraid to meet in crowds. The reality is that the pandemic is temporary, and must go away. Nevertheless, the world will continue to prepare for the potential, as well as take action to reduce long-term coronavirus disruption and accelerate speedier recovery. These were the few ideas to help hospitality resolve the difficulties COVID-19 carries with it. However, before such fundamental measures can be implemented, it will take a while, and even longer before they show impact. Restaurants, however, have the more pressing challenge of restoring confidence.

The hotels and restaurants are exploring whether to incorporate guidelines on grooming and psychological distancing. Of starters, businesses would focus much more on home deliveries than they used to. But it does need to include creative thought. Restaurants would have to invest in contactless logistics and create different menus for the delivery. They will also need to think more innovatively about packaging, since most of the time, online delivery packaging is just an afterthought. Many however think that concepts such as "contactless eating" have little real significance in hospitality. Going to a coffee shop or restaurant is a fundamentally social experience, and though people prefer time alone, they still go to stay in a coffee shop with the crowds, that's because it's convenient to have people around you.

However, there are still many unanswered questions regarding COVID-19, including those related to its impact on global hospitality. Therefore much remains to be studied regarding COVID-19 and tourism and hospitality, and results from such studies would be especially useful if a significant new epidemic and pandemic of the disease happens in the immediate future (or when, as forecast). Such research should also be of particular help in decision-making in the context of other crises which may still affect global hospitality industry.

References:

American Hotel & Lodging Association. (2020). Study Showcases Potential Negative Impact Of Coronavirus Pandemic on Hotel Industry Employment. AHLA. https://www.ahla.com/sites/default/files/fact_sheet_state_covid19_impacts_0.pdf

Asmelash, L., & Cooper, A. (2020, April 9). Nearly 80% of hotel rooms in the US are empty, according to new data. CNN. https://www.cnn.com/2020/04/08/us/hotel-rooms-industry-coronavirus-trnd/index.html

Bloom, D. E., & Cadarette, D. (2019). Infectious disease threats in the 21st Century: Strengthening the global response. Frontiers in Immunology, 10, 549. https://doi.org/10.3389/fimmu.2019.00549 [Crossref], [PubMed], [Web of Science ®]

Corkery, M., & Karni, A. (2020, January 31). Trump administration restricts entry into U.S. from China. The New York Times. https://www.nytimes.com/2020/01/31/business/china-travel-coronavirus.html

Department of Labor. (2020, April 9). COVID-19 Impact: Unemployment insurance weekly claims [Government]. Department of Labor. https://www.dol.gov/ui/data.pdf

European Centre for Disease Prevention and Control (ECDC). (2020). COVID-19 Situation update worldwide. Retrieved April 4, 2020, from https://www.ecdc.europa.eu/en/geographical-distribution-2019-ncov-cases

Fauci, A. S., & Morens, D. M. (2012). The perpetual challenge of infectious diseases. New England Journal of Medicine, 366(5), 454–461. https://doi.org/10.1056/NEJMra1108296 [Crossref], [PubMed], [Web of Science ®]

Franck, T., & Schoen, J. W. (2020, April 9). This map shows the states that suffered the biggest job losses last week due to coronavirus. CNBC. https://www.cnbc.com/2020/04/09/this-map-shows-the-states-that-suffered-the-biggest-job-losses-last-week-due-to-coronavirus.html

Gössling, S. (2002). Global environmental consequences of tourism. Global Environmental Change, 12(4), 283–302.

https://doi.org/10.1016/S0959-3780(02)00044-4

Hall, C. M. (2006). Tourism, biodiversity and global environmental change. In S. Gössling & C. M. Hall (Eds.), Tourism and global environmental change: Ecological, economic, social and political interrelationships (pp. 142–156). Routledge.

Hall, C. M. (2020). Biological invasion, biosecurity, tourism, and globalisation. In D. Timothy (Ed.), Handbook of globalisation and tourism (pp. 114–125). Edward Elgar.

Huang, C., Wang, Y., Li, X., Ren, L., Zhao, J., Hu, Y., Zhang, L., Fan, G., Xu, J., Gu, X., Cheng, Z., Yu, T., Xia, J., Wei, Y., Wu, W., Xie, X., Yin, W., Li, H., Liu, M., … Cao, B. (2020). Clinical features of patients infected with 2019 novel coronavirus in Wuhan. The Lancet, 395(10223), 497–506. https://doi.org/10.1016/S0140-6736(20)30183-5 [Crossref], [PubMed], [Web of Science ®]

Jonas, O. (2014). Pandemic risk. World Bank

Karmin, C. (2020, 19). Marriott begins furloughing tens of thousands of employees. Https://Www.Bangkokpost.Com. https://www.bangkokpost.com/business/1881850/marriott-begins-furloughing-tens-of-thousands-of-employees

Lindsey Kennett (2020). Survey estimates Virginia's restaurant, food service industry could lose $1.3 billion in April

National Academies of Sciences, Engineering, and Medicine. (2017). Global health and the future role of the United States. The National Academies Press.

National Academies of Sciences, Engineering, and Medicine. (2018). Understanding the economics of microbial threats: proceedings of a workshop. National Academies Press.

Ollila, J. (2020, February 14). Hilton Has Temporarily Closed 150 Hotels In China. Loyalty Lobby. https://loyaltylobby.com/2020/02/14/hilton-has-temporarily-closed-150-hotels-in-china/

Page, S., & Yeoman, I. (2007). How VisitScotland prepared for a flu pandemic. Journal of Business Continuity & Emergency Planning, 1(2), 167–182.

Reigler, P. (2020, March 18). Hilton to close most hotels in major cities. Frequent Business Traveler. http://www.frequentbusinesstraveler.com/2020/03/hilton-to-close-most-hotels-in-major-cities/

Scott, D., & Gössling, S. (2015). What could the next 40 years hold for global tourism? Tourism Recreation Research, 40(3), 269–285. https://doi.org/10.1080/02508281.2015.1075739 [Taylor & Francis Online], [Web of Science ®]

Simon Kutcher & Partners (2020) https://www.simon-kucher.com/en/resources/perspectives/new-normal-restaurants-consumer-behavior-world-after-covid-19-lockdowns

9

Published by S. Lock (2020) Number of employees in the restaurant industry in the U.S. 2010-2019

Toby Malbec (2020). Restaurant Business Model Changes in a Post COVID-19 World https://hospitalitytech.com/restaurant-business-model-changes-post-covid-19-world

Publisher: Eliva Press SRL

Email: info@elivapress.com

Eliva Press is an independent publishing house established for the publication and dissemination of academic works all over the world. Company provides high quality and professional service for all of our authors.

Our Services:
Free of charge, open-minded, eco-friendly, innovational.

-Free standard publishing services (manuscript review, step-by-step book preparation, publication, distribution, and marketing).
-No financial risk. The author is not obliged to pay any hidden fees for publication.
-Editors. Dedicated editors will assist step by step through the projects.
-Money paid to the author for every book sold. Up to 50% royalties guaranteed.
-ISBN (International Standard Book Number). We assign a unique ISBN to every Eliva Press book.
-Digital archive storage. Books will be available online for a long time. We don't need to have a stock of our titles. No unsold copies. Eliva Press uses environment friendly print on demand technology that limits the needs of publishing business. We care about environment and share these principles with our customers.
-Cover design. Cover art is designed by a professional designer.
-Worldwide distribution. We continue expanding our distribution channels to make sure that all readers have access to our books.

www.elivapress.com

Made in the USA
Columbia, SC
29 July 2021

42610491R00024